THE FACTS ON
HINDUISM
IN
AMERICA

John Ankerberg
& John Weldon

HARVEST HOUSE PUBLISHERS
Eugene, Oregon 97402

Other books by
John Ankerberg
and John Weldon

The Facts on Astrology
The Facts on the New Age Movement
The Facts on Spirit Guides
The Facts on the Masonic Lodge
The Facts on the Jehovah's Witnesses
The Facts on the Mormon Church
The Facts on False Teaching in the Church
The Facts on the Occult
The Facts on Islam

THE FACTS ON HINDUISM IN AMERICA

Copyright © 1991 by The Ankerberg
   Theological Research Institute
Published by Harvest House Publishers
Eugene, Oregon 97402

ISBN 0-89081-914-9

CONTENTS

The Guru Phenomenon

SECTION ONE
Introduction to Hinduism in America

SECTION TWO
The Common Practices of Hinduism in America

SECTION THREE
Hindu Theology in America

SECTION IV
Hinduism in America: A Critique

The Guru Phenomenon

> Once embarked on this [spiritual] journey,
> we are advised to seek the guidance of those
> who have been there before and know it well:
> teachers, gurus, roshis, swamis...and adepts
> of every description. But with common sense set
> aside, how can we judge the credentials of our
> teachers? What criteria can we use to deter-
> mine the suitability of this man or this woman
> to guide us along the path...?
>
> —*Yoga Journal* Editorial[1]

No one can underestimate the impact of Hinduism in America.* The purpose of this book is to evaluate the teachings and practices of many of the major Hindu gurus ("spiritual leaders") in America today. We will seek to determine whether the gurus constitute a positive or a negative religious and social force in modern America.

Why have we undertaken this study? Scores of lectures and many years of teaching reveal to us that considerable uncertainty and ignorance exists on the part of the public, including Christians, as to the potential implications and impact of the Hindu gurus' philosophy and practice. In the course of our research we also found this to be true for the large majority of the gurus' own disciples. We have written this booklet to remedy this unfortunate situation.

Why are the authors qualified to evaluate Hinduism in America? For two full years we have read through the important literature of the major gurus. We have held discussions and interviews with members of many different groups, consultations and discussions with leaders in the field of cults and new religions, and when possible visited sect headquarters both local and national. One of the authors of this book, Dr. Weldon, is a former practitioner of Eastern meditation and coauthor of a critique of one of the most popular forms of Hindu meditation in America, Transcendental Meditation. Dr. Weldon's Ph.D. was received in

---

* Hinduism in America is distinct from Hinduism in India in several ways; for example 1) Hindu influence in India pervades the entire culture; in America, Hinduism is one part of a larger religious culture; 2) the rampant idolatry (illustrated in thousands of temples and idols paraded throughout the streets of India) is currently lacking in America; 3) Hinduism in America is frequently "secularized," "Christianized," or otherwise toned down or made palatable for Western consumption. As examples we could cite a) Maharishi Mahesh Yogi's Hindu practice of Transcendental Meditation, which falsely claims it is a true science and not a religion, and b) the spiritistic revelation *A Course in Miracles*, which is merely Hinduism (advaita Vedanta) in "Christian" terms.

the field of comparative religion, with an emphasis on Eastern religion. His dissertation involved a 2500-page analysis of over 20 of the leading Hindu, Buddhist, and Sufi gurus operating in America.

Years of research have forced us to conclude that the individual claims of the gurus should be viewed critically, particularly their spiritual claims. Indeed, from the perspective of traditional Western values in general and Judeo-Christian philosophy and religion in particular, the American guru phenomenon constitutes a genuine threat to society, the family, morality, and the vitality of the church and her influence in culture.

Three major conclusions were arrived at from our study:

1. The guru phenomenon comprises a revival of occultic practice and philosophy. We repeatedly encountered themes of shamanism, spiritism, modified aspects of witchcraft practice, and other forms of paganism.

2. The gurus themselves often constitute an anti-Christian force; their religious instruction and practice does not lead to an alleged spiritual "enlightenment," but rather to harmful spiritual states and forces, including the distinct possibility of mental illness or demon possession.

3. The gurus are not divine incarnations as they claim, but are spiritually possessed occultists whose philosophical and occultic teachings possess serious consequences for human society and welfare.

In fact, had the average disciple of a Hindu guru known his true teachings—and the potential moral, psychological, and spiritual consequences of the Hindu path—we suspect that most would never have joined. After surveying some of the recent tragedies among followers of the gurus, even Dio Neff, a book-review editor for the *Yoga Journal*, is forced to wonder, "Are many Western seekers just fools?"[2]

SECTION ONE

Introduction to Hinduism in America

1. What is Hinduism?

In its most simple definition, Hinduism may be defined as the religious beliefs and practices common to India. Defining Hinduism in a more precise manner is difficult because of the wide number of practices and teachings it offers. To illustrate, we present selected definitions of Hinduism from authoritative sources:

> The Way of the majority of the people of India, a Way that is a combination of religious belief, rites, customs, and daily practices, many of which appear overtly secular but in most cases have religious origins and sanctions. Hinduism is noted as being the only one of the major beliefs that cannot be defined, for any definition is inadequate, contradictory, and incomplete.[3]

> The name used in the West to designate the traditional socioreligious structure of the Indian people. As a religion based on mythology, it has neither a founder (as do Buddhism, Islam, and Christianity) nor a fixed canon. Myriad local cults and traditions of worship or belief can be distinguished.[4]

> The variety of religious beliefs and practices making up the major religious tradition of the Indian subcontinent.[5]

> . . . a complex product of [the] amalgamation of various cults and beliefs within a common social framework [e.g., the caste system].[6]

But in spite of its diversity, Hinduism in general does reveal a number of common themes. Some of these include pantheism (the belief that All is God, God is All), polytheism (a belief in many lesser gods), and a reliance upon occultic ritual and practices.

2. How did Hinduism originate?

Hinduism originated from a body of conflicting and contradictory[7] literature called the *Vedas* (ca. 1500-1200 B.C.).

Hindus claim that this body of literature was supernaturally given by the Hindu gods. Thus these basic religious texts "make a special claim to be divine in their origin."[8]

The four Vedas are the *Rigveda*, *Samaveda*, *Yajurveda*, and *Artharvaveda*. They are divided into two parts: the "work" portion (basically polytheistic ritual) and the "knowledge" portion (philosophical speculation). This latter portion, the "knowledge" section, constitutes what is called the *Upanishads* or *Vedanta*: "Since they brought to a close each of the four Vedas, the Upanishads came to be spoken of often as the Vedanta—the *anta* or end of the Vedas."[9]

We stress again that the entire collection of Vedas is held to be supernaturally inspired: "The entire corpus of Vedic literature—the *Samhitas* and the exposition that came to be attached to them, the *Brahmanas*, the *Aranyakas* and the *Upanishads*—was considered *sruti* or divinely heard."[10]

Who was it that heard and received this supernatural inspiration? It was the Hindu *rishis* or *seers*—powerful occultists who interpreted their revelations as divine communication from the gods.[11]

But for reasons that will soon become clear, we cannot accept the idea that such literature had a *divine* origin. To the contrary, it bears all the marks of spiritistic inspiration.

3. How influential is Hinduism in modern America?

In all its forms, Hinduism has influenced tens of millions of people in America. By itself Maharishi Mahesh Yogi's Transcendental Meditation, a form of advaita Vedanta Hinduism, has over three million graduates.[12] Hinduism is influential on college campuses, in certain schools of psychology, such as the transpersonal school, and in a wide variety of religious movements.[13]

For example, the majority of several thousand transpersonal psychologists are involved in Eastern forms of meditation, and "one of the long-held goals of transpersonal psychology has been an integration of Western science and Eastern practice."[14]

The New Age movement, with a collective following in the millions, has also been powerfully influenced by Hinduism. For example, a popular New Age "bible," *A Course in Miracles*,* is basically a "Christianized" form of the religious philosophy taught by most Hindu gurus in America—

---

* For an evaluation of this spiritistic literature, see Ankerberg and Weldon, *Can You Trust Your Doctor? The Complete Guide to New Age Medicine*, Chapter 12.

advaita Vedanta. (See Question 5 for a discussion of this philosophy.)

In addition, there are literally scores of modern religious cults and sects that have been influenced by Hinduism to varying degrees. Below we supply some examples.

Werner Erhard is the founder of the controversial "est" and "The Forum" seminars, having almost one million graduates. Both est and The Forum were influenced by Hinduism through Swami Muktananda, one of Erhard's principal gurus.[15] The occult religion of Theosophy has also been influenced by Hinduism.[16] Many of the New Thought religions, such as Science of Mind and Divine Science, actively promote Hindu teachings. Mary Baker Eddy's Christian Science and Charles and Myrtle Fillmore's Unity School of Christianity were also influenced by Hinduism.[17] Much of the popular occultic religion of Eckankar is a plagiarism of a Hindu sect known as Radhasoami. Scientology, a powerful and controversial new religion, has also been influenced by Hinduism.[18]

In addition, literally tens of millions of Americans have taken up Hindu practices, such as yoga, meditation, developing altered states of consciousness, seeking Hindu "enlightenment," and various other occultic practices.

If we were to combine the influence of Hinduism in the guru movements, in American colleges, in the New Age movement, in religious practices such as yoga meditation, and in modern religious cultism, no one could deny that in various forms and ways Hinduism is influencing tens of millions of Americans.

4. Why do Americans need to be informed about Hinduism in America?

Americans should be informed about Hinduism because ignorance is widespread concerning its true practices and teachings. If Hinduism in America is often packaged as one thing when in fact it is something else entirely, then people have a right to that information.

5. What is the dominant Hindu belief in America?

In America the dominant Hindu belief is called *Vedanta*. Of all the conflicting schools of Hinduism, Vedanta has had the most profound overall influence:

> Vedanta ("the End of Vedas") was the school which gave organized and systematic form to the teaching of

the Upanishads. While the other schools are almost
or wholly extinct, Vedanta is still very much alive, for
nearly all the great Hindu religious teachers of recent
centuries have been Vedantists of one branch or
another.[19]

The influence of Vedanta on Indian thought has
been profound, so that it may be said that, in one or
another of its forms, Hindu philosophy has become
Vedanta.[20]

Hinduism is, truly speaking, the religion and philosophy of Vedanta.[21]

Since the texts of Vedanta are contradictory and impossible to interpret uniformly,[22] various schools of Vedanta
have arisen.

The dominant Vedantic school in America is called *advaita* or the "non-dual" school. This belief teaches that there
is only one impersonal God called *Brahman*. Brahman alone
is real; everything else is considered a dream of Brahman—
an "illusion."

This form of Hinduism teaches that as part of its "sport"
or "play" (*lila*), Brahman exuded or emerged the universe as
part of itself, but then "covered" it with what is called *maya*
or illusion. This illusion is the entire physical universe that
we see around us, including all stars and planets, the sky,
trees, rivers, mountains, and all people as well.[23]

However, Hinduism also teaches that Brahman exists
"beneath" this illusory universe. In other words, Brahman
resides "in" and "underneath" the material creation, including man. This explains why the goal of Hinduism is to
go inward to allegedly discover that one's true nature is part
of God or Brahman. Hinduism aims at supposedly revealing
one's inward divine nature by "contacting" Brahman through
occult practice.

This idea that the world is an illusion "hiding" Brahman
is a key teaching of Hinduism in America. As our next
questions will demonstrate, this teaching has profound
practical implications.

6. What are the beliefs of Hinduism concerning the world in which we live?

Because Hinduism teaches that the world is ultimately
an illusion, a "dream" of Brahman, the basic philosophy of
Hinduism can be described as nihilism. The *Oxford American Dictionary* defines nihilism as: "1) a negative doctrine,

the total rejection of current beliefs in religion or morals; 2) a form of skepticism that denies all existence."[24] Therefore, in the end Hindu practice leads to nihilism; e.g., "The experience of *samadhi* [Hindu "enlightenment"] is, literally, a death to the things of this world."[25]

Nihilism is exactly what the Hindu gurus in America teach.

Swami Vivekananda: The world... never existed; it was a dream, maya.[26]

Paramahansa Yogananda: I don't take life seriously at all.... It's all a dream.[27]

Ram Dass: What responsibility?... God has all the responsibility. I don't have any responsibility.[28]

Meher Baba: Mere mind and mere body do not exist.[29]

Da Free John: All of this life, past and future, up and down, in and out, is just an hallucination.... Birth, the world, and the whole affair of life become nonsense, no longer impinge on you, have no implication whatsoever, absolutely none.... Ultimately, there is no world.[30]

Bhagwan Shree Rajneesh: Your so-called society... is a conspiracy against man.... Whatever you call real life is not real.... Society is rotten.... I am not at all concerned with society.... [We are] escaping from illusions and escaping into reality [through "enlightenment"]—hence it's not really escapist.[31]

There is no purpose in life... the questions are meaningless, the answers are even more so... [life is a] meaningless, fruitless effort leading nowhere... this whole [life is] nonsense... you simply live: there is no purpose.[32]

Shree Aurobindo/The "Mother": One lives in Auroville [the spiritual community] in order to be free of moral and social conventions.[33]

According to Hinduism, Brahman is wholly indifferent to what goes on in the world. Brahman is *impersonal*; it does not speak and is unconcerned with good or evil. It is unconcerned with men and women. It has no cares because it has no feeling. It is unconcerned with morals because it has no values. Thus the one who "knows" Brahman knows that there is no right or wrong, nor is there a world in which they actually happen. In Hinduism the truly "enlightened" individual is indifferent to all actions, good or evil.

These are the beliefs of Hinduism in America concerning the world we live in: Ultimately the world we live in is an illusion, worth nothing.

Yet ironically, the Hindu gurus claim that they offer people a transcendence and "meaning" to life which Western materialism has cruelly denied them. In truth, however, both Hinduism and materialism end in exactly the same place—nihilism. This is why influential guru Da Free John asserts, "Upon this absolute Truth [of the despair of nihilism] we must build our lives."[34]

But switching to noted atheistic philosopher Bertrand Russell brings no change: "Only on the firm foundation of unyielding despair can the soul's habitation henceforth be safely built."[35]

Nevertheless, people who seriously adopt a nihilistic philosophy should realize that it can profoundly affect them. Consider the description of the truly "enlightened" soul as given by the great Hindu saint Ramakrishna:

> But the man who always sees God [Brahman] and talks to him intimately has an altogether different nature. He acts sometimes like an inert thing, sometimes like a ghoul, sometimes like a child, and sometimes like a madman.... He is not conscious of the holy and the unholy. He does not observe any formal purity. To him everything is Brahman.... People notice his ways and actions and think of him as insane.[36]

Any culture which adopts such a philosophy can also be profoundly affected. India is living proof that what a people are committed to inwardly is powerfully manifested outwardly. India's so-called "Wisdom from the East" carries a heavy price tag. A small part of this cost is discussed by Paul Molnar. Writing in the *National Review* he recalls his feelings after a trip to India:

> It was hard, afterward, to sort out my impressions, to pull them together. Paul Claudel once wrote to friends, during his travels and ambassadorships in the Far East, that oriental religion is the devil's invention. In these ecumenical times one is not supposed to say such things. Yet that is my inescapable conclusion. The faith of the worshippers is, without any doubt, sincere, even fervent.... But the objects of

worship are brutal, inhuman deities who know how to scare, punish, avenge, mock and cheat, not to elevate and forgive; and the environment surrounding the worshippers repels rather than attracts: horrid, grimacing idols with cunning or cruel stares; incredibly gaudy vulgarity, copulating monkeys, defecating cows, mud, stench, garbage. Hippies are drawn to this witches' brew, and the reason is not far to find.

What attracts and keeps them here is the degradation: of reason, of self-esteem, of vital forces, of faith in God and man. Here they find innumerable gods and none at all; everybody may do this thing just like the monkeys and the cows, sinking slowly toward the Ganges or Nirvana. Intelligence and purposefulness dissolve on the trashheap, the body rots until it becomes one with the road, the grass, the dung. The great nothingness envelops all, and the ashes go into the river.[37]

What gave India all this—and more? No one can deny that it was the religion of Hinduism, a religion that millions of Americans are now welcoming with open arms.

SECTION TWO

The Common Practices of Hinduism in America

7. The development of altered states of consciousness

In most Eastern practices, including those of Hinduism, the development of altered states of consciousness is encouraged. Millions of people today are pursuing such altered states, thinking that these will produce a condition of spiritual "enlightenment." Altered states can involve a variety of different experiences—everything from hypnosis and other trance states to yogic kundalini arousal [a technique of "enlightenment"], shamanism, lucid dreaming, drug states, meditation- and biofeedback-induced consciousness, etc.

But pursuing these states can be dangerous because altered states of consciousness also tend to open the doors to spirit possession. As we commented in another text:

> Historically the linkage between pagan cultures and the manipulation of consciousness for occult purposes, such as spirit possession, has been strong. This indicates that the spirit world has a vested interest in encouraging the exploration of altered states of consciousness along specific lines, especially those devoted to spirit contact.[38]

> Nobel scientist Sir John Eccles once commented that the human brain was "a machine that a ghost can operate." His statement illustrates the truth that given the proper conditions, the human mind can become an open door permitting the influence of spirits. Altered states of consciousness are one principal method offering the proper conditions.[39]

A major study on altered states of consciousness revealed that of almost 500 societies observed, over 90 percent considered the experience of trance states and spirit possession as being socially acceptable.[40] And now also in America, the influence of Hindu gurus and their occult practices are making trance and possession states socially acceptable. Today, in many quarters what was once called "spirit possession" is now simply termed "altered consciousness."

For example, consider the research of Tal Brooke, the former premier Western disciple of India's super guru Sathya Sai Baba. Brooke offers a powerful examination and critique of Eastern philosophy, including the altered states of consciousness found in the meditative disciplines of endless numbers of gurus. Altered states of consciousness are revealed as potential ways to foster spirit contact and possession.[41] Yet those who experience spirit possession frequently define it merely as an "altered state" of consciousness.

In conclusion, when Hindu gurus claim that their yogic/ meditative practices will produce a "higher" state of consciousness, the practitioner should beware. As we have documented elsewhere, these meditation-induced altered states can easily lead to periods of social withdrawal, mental illness and even demonization.[42]

8. The practices of yoga and meditation

Other typical practices of Hinduism include the interrelated disciplines of yoga and meditation. Due to space restrictions, we will limit our discussion to yoga, keeping in mind that true yoga practice involves meditation. (See note 42.)

Over the years more and more health professionals have advocated yoga as a "safe and effective" method for procuring physical and mental health. Today, literally millions of people in America trust this ancient Hindu practice.

True yoga has one specific goal: unite the person to Brahman through experiences of mystical consciousness. The individual is to realize that he is one essence with God—i.e., Brahman itself: "The aim of yoga, then, is to achieve the state of unity or oneness with God, Brahman, [and] spiritual beings [spirits]...."[43] Yoga authority Gopi Krishna observes, "All the systems of yoga...are designed to bring about those psychosomatic [mental and physical] changes in the body which are essential for the metamorphosis [change] of consciousness"[44] that is required to "realize" Brahman.

This is why yoga authorities confess that yogic postures and breathing practices awaken occultic energies and psychic powers that can finally lead to dramatic changes in consciousness—changes so powerful that many people are forever altered by them. (For example, see note 41.)

Although many Americans practice yoga as mere exercise, few have any idea of where such practice may take them. In the literature we have read numerous accounts of yoga-induced insanity and demonization even from innocent yoga practice. But incredibly, the altered states that yoga produces—even the periods of madness—are now frequently defined as positive spiritual experiences, capable of leading one to spiritual "enlightenment."[45]

That yoga practice can break down the mind and body is not surprising. The very goal of yoga is to *destroy* the person (who is only a false self, an illusion) so that the impersonal Brahman (the alleged Real Self) may be experienced.

Moti Lal Pandit observes that:

> ...the aim of Yoga is to realize liberation from the human condition. To achieve this liberation, various psychological, physical, mental, and mystical [occult] methods have been devised. All those methods are anti-social (sometimes even anti-human) in that yoga prescibes a way of life which says: "This mortal life is not worth living."[46]

Because yoga is ultimately an occult practice (e.g., it characteristically develops psychic abilities), it is not unexpected that the characteristic hazards of occult practice—

e.g., physical diseases, mental illness, and demonization[47]—could be encountered. We believe that these hazards are encountered *because yoga is an occult practice* and not because yoga is allegedly performed in an incorrect manner.

Most people (including most medical doctors) wrongly assume that yoga is harmless. They rarely consider yoga per se as relevant to any illnesses they may encounter in their patients. But we are convinced that many perplexing conditions, including some deaths, are related to yoga. For example, Swami Prabhavananda warns about the dangers of yogic breathing exercises:

> Now we come to breathing exercises. Let me caution you: they can be very dangerous. Unless properly done, there is a good chance of injuring the brain. And those who practice such breathing without proper supervision can suffer a disease which no known science or doctor can cure. It is impossible even for a medical person to diagnose such an illness.[48]

Many yoga authorities openly confess the dangers of yoga practice. As noted, these dangers are often said to arise from "wrong" methods. But in fact no one has ever objectively identified the specific mechanics of "correct" or "incorrect" yoga; "incorrect" yoga practice in one tradition is often "correct" practice in another.[49] Below we cite some of the hazards of yoga as noted by yoga authorities.

Shree Purohit Swami's commentary on Pantanjali's *Yoga Sutras* warns:

> In India and Europe, I came across some three hundred people who suffered permanently from wrong practices. The doctors, upon examination, found there was nothing organically wrong and consequently could not prescribe treatment.[50]

United Nations spiritual adviser and spiritist[51] Sri Chinmoy, author of *Yoga and the Spiritual Life*, observes: "To practice *pranayama* [yogic breath control] without real guidance is very dangerous. I know of three persons who have died from it...."[52]

Yoga authority Hans-Ulrich Rieker admonishes in *The Yoga of Light*: "Yoga is not a trifling jest if we consider that any misunderstanding in the practice of yoga can mean death or insanity," and that in *kundalini* yoga, if the breath or *prana* is "prematurely exhausted [withdrawn] there is immediate danger of death for the yogi."[53]

Gopi Krishna, another yoga authority, also warns of the possible dangers of yoga practice, including "drastic effects" on the central nervous system and the possibility of death.[54]

The standard authority on Hatha yoga, *The Hatha Yoga Pradipika* (chapter 2, verse 15), cautions: "Just as lions, elephants, and tigers are tamed, so the *prana* [breath; actually *prana* is the alleged divine energy underlying the breath] should be kept under control. Otherwise it can kill the practitioner."[55]

Hindu master Sri Krishna Prem cautions in *The Yoga of the Bhagavat Gita*: "As stated before, nothing but dangerous, mediumistic psychisms or neurotic dissociations of personality can result from the practice of [yoga] meditation without the qualifications mentioned at the end of the last chapter."[56] He warns, "To practice it, as many do, out of curiosity...is a mistake which is punished with futility, neurosis, or worse ["even insanity itself"]."[57]

Swami Prabhavananda's *Yoga and Mysticism* lists brain injury, incurable diseases, and insanity as potential hazards of wrong yoga practice;[58] Rieker lists cancer of the throat, all sorts of ailments, blackouts, strange trance states, or insanity from even "the slightest mistake...."[59]

In *The Seven Schools of Yoga*, Ernest Wood warns of "the imminent risk of most serious bodily disorder, disease, and even madness."[60]

In conclusion, if yoga teachers were more frank concerning their methods, perhaps we would hear less of the "yoga is perfectly safe" propaganda.

9. The practice of attaining "enlightenment"

The goal of Hinduism is to attain "enlightenment"— alleged realization of one's inner nature as God. As noted, the typical means to this realization involve the cultivation of abnormal states of consciousness through yoga and meditation practice. In later questions we discuss why we believe that the Hindu practice of enlightenment is a dangerous practice which may ultimately lead to mental illness and/or demonization. (See Questions 17-20.)

10. The practice of occultism

Hinduism is an occult religion. Hinduism began from occultic practice and the supernatural revelations given to the *rishis* or seers. Considering the American gurus as a whole, it is not surprising that occult practices are widely accepted. Typically they include not only various forms of spiritism but also astrology, magic, sorcery, necromancy, development of psychic abilities, shamanistic practices, the transferal of occult power in initiation (*shaktipat diksha*), etc.

As veteran researcher Brooks Alexander observes of Rajneesh, Muktananda, and Sai Baba:

> All of these gurus espouse a similar philosophy, and they all turn it into practice in a similar way. It is a pattern that we find not only in tantra (Indo-Tibetan occultism), but in European satanism, antinomian gnosticism, and ancient pagan sorcery as well.[61]

Rajneesh, for example, states that witchcraft constitutes "one of the greatest possibilities of human growth."[62]

Part of the disciples' required obedience to the guru is to follow the guru's *sadhana* or spiritual path. By definition this places a person on the path of occultism. In fact, psychic powers[63] and spiritism are to be expected. For example, spirit contact frequently occurs with what are believed to be various Hindu deities, "nature" spirits, or the guru himself after death (or even while alive via his alleged "spiritual form"). Muktananda tells us his students encounter various Hindu gods and other spirits as well as the dead.[64]

Paramahansa Yogananda's spiritual autobiography, *Autobiography of a Yogi*, is replete with occult experiences—astral projection, psychometry, astrology, psychic healing, spiritistic materializations and apportations, amulets, etc.[65] For example, Yogananda teaches, "True spiritualism [mediumism] is a wonderful science ... it is possible by meditation and spiritual [occult] development to contact departed loved ones...."[66]

The text *Sri Aurobindo and the Mother on Occultism* claims that true occultism is "dynamic spirituality ... an indispensable instrument along the spiritual path."[67] Aurobindo and the "Mother" emphasize that "to talk about occult things is of little value; one must experience them."[68]

When the gurus endorse occult practices such as spirit contact, mediumism, divination, astrology, and necromancy (contacting the dead), they are expressly violating God's instructions warning against such things: "Let no one be found among you ... who practices divination or sorcery ... engages in witchcraft, or casts spells, or who is a medium or spiritist or who consults the dead. Anyone who does these things is detestable to the Lord ..." (Deuteronomy 18:10-12).

SECTION THREE

Hindu Theology in America

11. *What does Hinduism believe about God?*

Hinduism in America teaches that God is an impersonal divine essence they call Brahman. Brahman has two aspects, one that is called "Nirguna" and another that is called "Saguna." The technical distinctions between these "forms" of Brahman are too detailed to discuss here (see footnote 23). For our purposes we can state that Hinduism in America teaches that everything is God or part of God.[69] This is known as pantheism.

In *The Gospel of Sri Ramakrishna* we read, "It is God Himself [Brahman] who has become all this—the [physical] universe, maya [the illusion] and the living beings.... It is God alone who has become everything."[70] Thus Hinduism teaches that "there is nothing that is not God."[71]

Nevertheless, because the Hindu concept of God involves so many contradictions, Hindus have ultimately concluded that nothing concrete can be said about God. Thus, "no one has ever been able to say what Brahman is."[72] Further, "the nature of Brahman cannot be described. About it one remains silent."[73] The common phrase used by Hindus to describe Brahman is "Neti Neti"—"not this, not that."

The Hindu God is also impersonal: "The idea of a Personal God is not a true generalization. We have to go beyond, to the Impersonal [God]...the Personal God...is not absolute truth."[74]

Hinduism also teaches that Brahman can be neither known nor worshiped: "God in His absolute [nirguna] nature is not to be worshiped. Worshiping such a God would be nonsense.... It would be sin to worship that God."[75]

In *Teachings of Swami Vivekananda*, we are informed that Brahman does not know anything. He is described as—

> ... an impersonal, omnipresent being who cannot be called a knowing being.... He cannot be called a thinking being, because that [i.e., thinking] is a process of the weak only. He cannot be called a reasoning being, because reasoning is a sign of weakness. He

cannot be called a creating being, because none creates except in bondage.[76]

Thus the ultimate God of Hinduism in America is 1) pantheistic, 2) impersonal, 3) unknowing, and 4) unknowable. It cannot love or show mercy because love and mercy are personal attributes. It cannot know or be known because these are also attributes of personality. In conclusion, what Brahman is or isn't no one knows, because the descriptions of It are contradictory.

By contrast, the biblical God is personal, loving, and holy. He *can* be known and experienced personally. Because He is personal, and because we are created in His image, our personhood has meaning and dignity. There is no need to view ourselves as illusions or to seek to destroy our personhood in order to "reach" Brahman. (See Question 18.)

The Bible also teaches that God is a God who loves. In fact, the Bible teaches that "God is love" (1 John 4:8).

Nowhere is God's love better demonstrated than at the cross, where He took on human nature and, in one act of unparalleled self-denial, took all the world's sins upon Himself and was judged in our place. He did this because of His great love for mankind and His desire that no one should perish (Philippians 2:1-8; John 3:16; 2 Peter 3:9). But in Hinduism such ideas are rejected as illustrations of spiritual ignorance. (See Question 14.)

12. What does Hinduism believe about man?

Hinduism in America teaches that man outwardly (his body and personality) is an illusion. But in his true inward nature he is one essence with Brahman. The common phrase used to describe this assumption is "Atman is Brahman." In other words, the individual human soul, *atman*, is ultimately one essence with *Brahman*. Here are some representative teachings.

Muktananda explains, "The Guru is God Himself...."[77] Thus, "Muktananda ... is the God of the universe."[78] Further, "As you worship God, you become God...."[79] cf. 80

Swami Satchidananda refers to our "true nature which is God."[81]

Sai Baba teaches, "You are the God of this universe."[82] Further, he emphasizes, "You *are* God in reality"[83] and "You are not a man, you are God...."[84]

Rajneesh emphasizes, "As you are, you are God."[85]

The following is a typical yoga meditation intended to help the disciple realize that he really is God. It is given by Swami Vishnudevananada:

I am the light of lights; I am the sun; I am the real, real, sun.... In me the whole world moves and has its being.... I existed before the world began.... I permeate and pervade every atom.... Oh, how beautiful I am.... I am the whole universe; everything is in me.... I am That [Brahman]."[86]

But the Bible teaches that this philosophy is wrong. In his own heart every person knows he is not God. Man is a creation of God, not God Himself: "So God created man in his own image, in the image of God he created him; male and female he created them" (Genesis 1:27). "The Sovereign Lord says: 'In the pride of your heart you say, "I am a god; I sit on the throne of a god.... But you are man and not a god, though you think you are as wise as a god'" (Ezekiel 28:2).

The Bible also teaches that the true inner nature of man is not divine, but sinful: "From within, out of men's hearts, come evil thoughts, sexual immorality, theft, murder, adultery, greed, malice, deceit, lewdness, envy, slander, arrogance and folly" (Mark 7:21-23). Men are not to look to themselves inwardly for salvation. Instead, they are to look to God, their Creator, for salvation. "This is what the Lord says: 'Cursed is the one who trusts in man, who depends on flesh for his strength and whose heart turns away from the Lord'" (Jeremiah 17:5). In conclusion, what the Bible has said is *God's creation* (mankind) Hinduism has said is *God Itself.* What the Bible has said is *sinful and imperfect* (fallen human nature) Hinduism has said is *divine.*

13. What does Hinduism believe about Jesus?

The Hindu gurus typically redefine Jesus after their own likeness. Jesus becomes a teacher of Hinduism, a guru of the past who has been greatly misunderstood by Christians. Thus the only Jesus the gurus praise is a Hindu Jesus. The biblical Jesus is either ignored or ridiculed—or even condemned as a false Christ. Rajneesh teaches:

To tell you the truth, Jesus is a mental case.... He is a fanatic. He carries the same kind of mind as Adolf Hitler. He is a fascist. He thinks that only those who follow *him* will be saved.... And the fools are still believing that they will be saved if they follow Jesus. Even Jesus is not saved. And he knew it.[87]

Now Jesus is just a salesman, saying, "Come follow me, because those who will follow me will find God, and will find heaven."...Now, this man is not going to help anybody....[88]

Swami Vivekananda asserts, "The Trinitarian Christ is elevated above us; the Unitarian Christ is merely a mortal man. Neither can help us."[89] And, "Every worm is the brother of the Nazarene....The range of idols is from wood and stone to Jesus and Buddha."[90]

Da Free John emphasizes that the Jesus of Christian faith is a cultic "false idol" and "a perversion of the truth."[91] [92]

But what Hinduism teaches about Jesus Christ is wrong. Jesus never taught He was a Hindu guru; He taught He was the promised Jewish Messiah[93] and the only incarnation of God ever to appear—the "one and only" Son of God (John 3:16-18; cf. John 5:18). Jesus claimed He was God (John 10:30; 14:9; 19:7) and proved it by rising from the dead. In all of history, no Hindu guru has ever risen from the dead. The entire New Testament emphasizes that Jesus Christ is God Himself: "In Christ all the fullness of the Deity lives in bodily form..." (Colossians 2:9). Christians everywhere "wait for the blessed hope—the glorious appearing of our great God and Savior, Jesus Christ..." (Titus 2:13).

Jesus is not some guru from the past, dead and gone. The Bible teaches that Jesus is alive now and exalted above everything. Because of His atoning death on the cross and resurrection—

> God exalted him to the highest place and gave him the name that is above every name, that at the name of Jesus every knee should bow, in heaven and on earth and under the earth, and every tongue confess that Jesus Christ is Lord, to the glory of God the Father (Philippians 2:9-11).

And—

> He is the image of the invisible God, the firstborn over all creation. For by him all things were created: things in heaven and on earth, visible and invisible, whether thrones or powers or rulers or authorities; all things were created by him and for him. He is before all things, and in him all things hold together (Colossians 1:15-17).

In conclusion, the Hindu gurus reject the biblical Jesus Christ when they deny His nature (the unique God-Man) and mission (atoning Savior).

14. What does Hinduism believe about salvation ("enlightenment")?

Hinduism defines salvation as 1) the realization of our own Godhood, 2) the progressive "working out" of that realization throughout our life, and 3) the final merging with—a complete dissolution into—the impersonal God Brahman. This process may require millions of lifetimes as we strive to earn our own salvation by working off our "karma" ("unenlightened" thoughts and actions) in accordance with Hindu requirements.

For example, Hinduism teaches that all men and women are now living in great delusion. They think this world is ultimately real when it is only a dream. This delusion leads them into false perceptions, harmful ideas, and destructive ways of living—in other words, to adding more and more "karma" to one's life. Hinduism thus seeks to save them from this great deception.

The goal of Hindu salvation is therefore an alleged "enlightenment"—a denial of the world as it is and the "realization" of spiritual reality as Hinduism defines it. As we have seen, a key part of that realization is that the world is an illusion and that in our true nature we are God.

But if one is already God, then to seek a God outside oneself is foolish and spiritually destructive. One must turn inward, not outward. This is why Rajneesh teaches, "The greatest deception is the deception of devotion to God."[94] In other words, men and women must be devoted to themselves, for they are God inwardly; they must not be devoted to an independent Creator God, a false idol they think exists apart from them. According to Hinduism, this will only damage them spiritually.

The Bible teaches something entirely different about salvation. It teaches that men and women are sinful and require *redemption* (forgiveness of sins), not so-called "enlightenment." If any person's sins are not forgiven in this life, he will pay the divine penalty and judgment on his sins after death—eternal separation from God. This is why Jesus Christ came to earth. At the cross, Jesus was judged by God in our place (1 Peter 2:23; 1 John 2:2). God did this because He loves us and does not desire that anyone perish.

In Christianity, salvation is a free gift that God offers all people who will confess their sinfulness before Him, acknowledge that Christ died for their sins on the cross, and then receive Christ as their personal Savior: "The wages of sin is death, but the gift of God is eternal life in Christ Jesus our

Lord" (Romans 6:23). "To all who received him, to those who believed in his name, he gave the right to become children of God . . ." (John 1:12). "It is by grace you have been saved, through faith—and this not from yourselves, it is the gift of God—not by works, so that no one can boast" (Ephesians 2:8,9).

15. What does Hinduism believe about life after death?

The basic teaching of Hinduism concerning the afterlife involves a belief in reincarnation, the idea that we have many lifetimes to perfect ourselves, to work off our "karma" (spiritual imperfections) until we finally merge back into Brahman. Tens of millions of Americans believe in reincarnation today largely because of the influence of Hinduism and other forms of occult practice.

For example, there are thousands of reports of alleged "past lives" episodes being experienced by different people. These episodes have convinced many that reincarnation is true.

Nevertheless, after an in-depth investigation into reincarnation, we see no genuine evidence to support such a belief. Further, we are convinced that "past-life" experiences are really self-deceptions or even demonic deceptions— hypnotic-like experiences which cause people merely to *think* they have lived before.

We are not alone in our convictions. Probably the leading secular reincarnation researcher in America is parapsychologist Ian Stevenson of the University of Virginia. Although sympathetic to the idea, he denies that there is any proof of reincarnation and also accepts that one explanation for reincarnation experiences is that they are implanted into the mind by deceiving spirits.[95] Further, this is the conclusion of many Christian scholars who have studied reincarnation, such as Walter Martin, Mark Albrecht, John Synder, Robert Morey, Norman Geisler, and J. Yutaka Amano.[96]

In fact, we have yet to encounter a claimed reincarnation experience that is not best explained by recourse to natural theories or demonic power and deception.

Why would demons be interested in encouraging a belief in reincarnation? Simply because it is such an effective barrier to the Christian gospel. If people live through many lifetimes, then there is no biblical judgment at death—as Hebrews 9:27 teaches. If people must work out their own salvation over many lifetimes, then Christ did not have to die on the cross for our sins—as 1 John 2:2 and Luke 24:25,26 teach. If all people will eventually be saved and absorbed into the impersonal Brahman, then there is no eternal heaven or hell—as Matthew 25:46 and Revelation 20:10-15 teach.

These and many other factors reveal why it is logical to conclude that the teaching of reincarnation involves spiritual deception.

SECTION FOUR

Hinduism in America: A Critique

In this section we will briefly address some of the consequences of Hindu practice in America.

16. Should gurus be obeyed whether right or wrong?

A characteristic common to most cults is that the guru or leader requires unquestioning obedience on the part of the disciple. The disciple is to obey the guru just as he would obey God. Disobedience is cause for immediate expulsion from the spiritual community.

The following statements are illustrative.

Sri Aurobindo: There must be total and sincere surrender. . . . The surrender must be total.[97]

Bhagwan Shree Rajneesh: You are nobody to judge what is right and what is wrong. . . . This is none of your business. . . . Whatsoever I decide is absolute. If you don't choose that way you are perfectly happy to leave.[98]

Sai Baba: I will insist on strict obedience.[99]

Meher Baba: I am for the selected few who . . . surrender their all, body, mind and possessions to me. Those who have today willingly chosen to become my slaves will become true masters tomorrow.[100]

It is frightening to realize that some followers of Eastern gurus have frankly admitted that they would do anything, even commit murder or suicide, if their guru told them to.[101] This is because the disciple must never hesitate or question the will of the guru. If the guru is God, then the guru must be obeyed *as* God.

Da Free John teaches:

> When I approach you, I ask you for this, I ask you for that.... I ask you for everything. The longer you stay with me, the more things I will ask you for. I will ask you for *all of it*. You must yield everything to me. You must yield yourself in every function. Your very cells must yield. Only then are you fit for the Divine Yoga....[102]

Obeying the guru "right or wrong" is made easier because of another teaching. The Hindu gurus instruct their disciples that their *mind* is their enemy. If they desire true "liberation," the mind must be "destroyed." We examine this bizarre teaching in our next question.

17. Is the mind our enemy?

According to the gurus, the human mind is not a gift from God. Rather, it is a form of spiritual poison. The mind and its normal thoughts are trapped in delusions. Because the mind perceives only falsehoods, it is really our spiritual enemy and must be undermined to permit the experiencing of "higher" consciousness. Thus logic, common sense, and reason are rejected as "lower" forms of consciousness that prevent allegedly more spiritual forms of "knowing."

Normal consciousness is equated with spiritual ignorance or being "unenlightened." Because spiritual truth is allegedly understood only in an altered state of consciousness, specific spiritual (occult) techniques (yoga, meditation, etc.) are the means to the needed "restructuring" of the mind. Below we present selected illustrations of the gurus' teachings.

Bhagwan Shree Rajneesh:

> I am for the death of [the] mind....[103]

> I'm not here to strengthen your mind. I'm here to destroy it.... Much will have to be done to destroy your mind.[104]

> If you go on nourishing the mind, you are poisoning yourself.... The mind becomes almost like a cancerous growth.[105]

Sai Baba:

> [You must achieve] elimination of the mind, which is the arch obstacle in the [spiritual] path.[106]
>
> Do not listen to your mind [but] ... to my voice. ...[107]
>
> Give [your minds] to me ... but it must be a complete handing over; no reservations; the mind is the source of delusion.[108]

Meher Baba:

> As long as the mind is there, the real "I am God" state cannot be experienced.... Therefore... [the] mind must go.... Mind has to destroy itself.... The mind has to die in this body... [We must] attain this... annihilation of the mind during this life.[109]

Aurobindo:

> We can do very well without the mind ... in truth, we are the better for it.[110]

Radhasoami (Charan Singh, Sawan Singh, Swami Ji):

> Our mind leads us astray.[111]
>
> Fear the devil, your own mind.[112]

But should anyone be surprised that a rejection of the mind as one's "enemy" might produce an irrational approach to life? In her critique of Hindu spirituality, *Karma Cola: The Marketing of the Mystic East*, Indian author Gita Mehta observes the following of those who travel East in search of alleged "wisdom":

> The early Christian missionaries were not paranoid. Heathens do dabble in the irrational, and none more elaborately than Indian heathens, who have in their long evolution spent a couple of thousand years cultivating the transcendence of reason, another couple of thousand years on the denial of reason, and even more millennia on accepting reason, but rejecting its authenticity. To be cast adrift in this whirlpool of differing views on the validity of simple mental activity seems a very high price to pay for cheap air fares.[113]

Thus, not unexpectedly, even the gurus frequently confess to their own irrationalism.

Bhagwan Shree Rajneesh:

> What I am doing here is absurd, it is not logical. You will have to put logic aside....[114]

> Many times you will find my statements contradictory—they are contradictory, they are absurd because I will say one thing one moment and I will contradict it another moment....I am only consistent in one thing—my inconsistencies....[115]

> The energy of love and hate...are one energy... [hate] is not a different thing [than love].[116]

Maharishi Mahesh Yogi:

> It is only childish and ridiculous to base one's life on the level of thinking. Thinking can never be a profound basis of living. Being [living in "higher" consciousness] is the natural basis [of living]....Thinking, on the other hand, is only imaginary.[117]

Unfortunately, rejecting the mind is only the *first* step on the road to "enlightenment."

18. Is personhood something to be destroyed?

As we have seen, Hinduism in America frequently teaches that the individual person (body, mind, personality, etc.) is a false self that has no ultimate reality. Since Hinduism teaches that the only true reality is the impersonal God Brahman and that the entire creation is an illusion, then the individual *person* must *also* be considered an illusion.[118] In fact, it is the individual *person* that is the enemy of spiritual enlightenment. This is why the goal of most Hindu and Buddhist practice is to destroy *the person* so that one's alleged inner, *impersonal* divine reality may "emerge" and be revealed. But there are at least three consequences to this teaching.

First, this Hindu methodology is finally reduced to an assault upon the image of God in man, an image that is clearly personal. It seeks to destroy that which God Himself has created and has also identified as something good (Genesis 1:31).

Second, what replaces the reamed-out human personality is, paradoxically, often a new personality—an evil spirit which the Bible identifies as a demon. Thus what is incorrectly interpreted as something "demonic" (the person) is finally replaced by that which truly is demonic (an evil spirit). We discuss this in Question 20.

Third, whenever this process of alleged "enlightenment" involves physical or spiritual brutality, a convenient rationalization is ready-made: No genuine harm is perpetrated since no true person exists to be harmed. Below we provide examples.

Bhagwan Shree Rajneesh:

> You have been thinking that you are something unique, something special . . . you are nobody.[119]

> To me the person does not exist. . . . The person is nonexistent, a nonentity. . . .[120]

> As you are you cannot become enlightened. Great chunks of your being will have to be cut and thrown away. It will be almost like committing suicide.[121]

Da Free John:

> But the process in which the guru involves you in the meantime is destroying the separate self-sense and destroying the viewpoint of conventional cognition and perception.[122]

In other words, the path of Hinduism involves a destruction of the disciple by one who has already been destroyed himself—that is, the guru or "enlightened" spiritual master. Thus the path of yoga is acknowledged as "a progressive dismantling of human personality ending in a complete abolition. With every step of Yoga what we call 'man' is demolished a little more."[123] This is why Rajneesh teaches, "I am going to destroy you *utterly*. Only then can I help you."[124]

In fact, the purpose of the destruction is a temporary insanity that allows a new "mind" to emerge:

> A master is utterly destructive; a Master creates a chaos. He drives you insane as far as your mind is concerned—because when the mind has been driven insane, it stops . . . and suddenly a new consciousness arises.[125]

This is why Rajneesh confesses that "around great Masters you will see many people who look like zombies. [This is] something immensely valuable."[126]

According to Da Free John, everything that attaches us to our separate individual, personal existence must be annihilated:

> Among devotees there are no marriages, there are no brothers, sisters, husbands, wives, mothers, fathers, cousins, karmic friends, there is none of that. All of that is obsolete.... Spiritual life is leading to the absolute undermining of your separate existence. Absolutely. That is what this work is all about.... You are not going to go to heaven from here. You are going to die: literally and absolutely.[127]

Da Free John, who presumably experienced "enlightenment" himself, proceeds to inform his disciples that all "contracts" (contracts constitute our beliefs about many things—personal morals, standards, relationships, marriage, etc.) must deliberately be violated and undermined:

> One of the "secrets" of spiritual life is continually to violate your own contracts. If you do that with intelligence, with understanding, you will continually be free...do not assume any contracts to be invalid. Do not assume any contracts to hold.[128]

In the words of a devoted disciple, Da Free John provides the following advice to his spiritual students:

> But the maturity that the disciple's sadhana [path] requires is a matter of becoming grounded enough in the life of Satsang [spiritual growth] that the guru can begin to really throw you around, undermine you, disorient you to the point of the absolute impossibility of any form of orientation whatsoever. That is what God-Realization amounts to. *You* disappear, along with every vestige of your attempts to make sense out of existence. Bubba once described looking forward to the appearance of his first disciples so that he could start to really "punch heads"![129]

No one should doubt that this destruction of the personality can be frighteningly real—or that such destruction (in reaming out the original personality) can open the door for the body to be inhabited by a new and foreign personality. If God's gift of personhood is rejected and tossed away as so much garbage, and if the human mind is deliberately emptied and becomes a vacuum, then we should not be surprised that the "new consciousness" that enters and fills the vacuum could be something unexpected—even something evil.

19. Is morality a reflection of unenlightened consciousness?

Charles Manson once stated, "If God is One, what is bad?" Hinduism teaches that "God is One"—that ultimate reality is One impersonal, undifferentiated divine essence. What this means is that just as humanity itself is ultimately meaningless (as separate individual persons) then humanity's morality must also be meaningless. Human morality is simply a product of "unenlightened" and "deluded" thinking; morality per se does not exist.

Thus in Hinduism in America we often find not only the rejection of the image of God in man concerning his personality, but also the attempt to defile the image of God in man concerning his morality—his conscience. "Moral" thinking is held to be as destructive of "higher" consciousness and true reality as any other binding and illusory activity.

But if we really believe that man as man is only an illusion, and that morality is irrelevant, then is it surprising to discover that those who hold such views are willing to accept the mistreatment, brutalization, or even demonization of other men and women?

While few disciples live these spiritual "truths" consistently, this Hindu philosophy can become the means to justify selfish, unethical, immoral, cruel, or evil behavior, particularly on the part of the guru who can view such actions through any number of alleged rationalizations.

The guru may justify his evil on the basis of his claimed inability to commit evil, or its ultimate nonexistence, or his own divine authority, or as a spiritual "test" for the sake of the disciples' spiritual "growth" in apprehending metaphysical "truth" (e.g., that evil has no reality).

Virtually any evil, from deliberate deception to criminal activity, is capable of rationalization within such a monistic ("All is One") system. Thus "What you would normally think to be right or wrong no longer has any place. The underlying premise is that everything that the guru does is for your own good. The guru does no wrong."[130]

If morality is ultimately part of the illusion of Brahman, then to achieve true enlightenment, to inhabit true Reality, one must go beyond the idea of good and evil. Theoretically, once a disciple becomes truly enlightened, any actions, even evil actions, become "spiritual" actions, since the "enlightened" person is by definition incapable of committing evil. He cannot possibly commit that which does not exist.

Swami Muktananda:

> Our concepts of sin and virtue . . . alienate us from our true Self. . . . That which you see as impure is pure. . . . You imagine [ideas of] sin and virtue through ignorance.[131]

Swami Satchidananda:

> If you are possessed by that higher sense of wisdom, nothing is bad.[132]

Paramahansa Yogananda:

> [God] sees your good and evil thoughts and actions but they do not matter to him.[133]

Bhagwan Shree Rajneesh:

> My ashram [spiritual community] makes no difference between the Devil and the Divine. . . . I use all sorts of energies. And if the devilish energy can be used in a divine way, it becomes tremendously fruitful.[134]

> Obedience [to God] is the greatest sin.[135]

> I don't believe in morality . . . and I am bent on destroying it. . . . I believe in consciousness, not conscience.[136]

> The person who has deep compassion is not going to be bothered about whether he tells a lie or a truth. . . . All [spiritual teachers] have lied. . . . Through lies, by and by a master brings you toward light.[137]

> To emphasize morality is mean, degrading; it is inhuman.[138]

Da Free John:

> Divine life itself . . . is entirely separate from all of the usual moralistic [expletive deleted].[139]

Swami Adbhutananda:

> Good and evil have no absolute reality.[140]

Swami Vivekananda:

> Really, good and evil are one and the same.[141]

Given the above teachings no one should be surprised when they hear of gurus or their disciples caught in immoral or even criminal behavior. Rajneesh teaches, "[homosexual love] is natural . . . far easier, far more convenient."[142] Da Free John teaches, "It is not suggested that homosexuals in the ashram abandon their sexual life."[143] He also teaches, "Sex relations are [a divine process, in or out of marriage] . . . a random and loving occasion without [any] contracts [obligations]."[144] Even in light of the modern AIDS plague, the teachings of some gurus concerning sexual permissiveness continue.

Most people today entertain the common misconception that the gurus live morally celibate lives. However, our own research and that of others indicates that most are not celibate, even when they claim they are. The research of Buddhist teacher and psychologist Jack Kornfield, as given in "Sex Lives of the Gurus," reveals:

> Deception has proven to be the greatest source of disappointment and pain in spiritual groups. The discovery of covert or inapproapriate sexual relations between teachers and students is not an infrequent occurrence. In recent years such discoveries have caused major upheavals in nearly a dozen of the largest Eastern spiritual communities in America.[145]

Of 54 gurus examined, 39 were found to be sexually active—over 70 percent. Close to 90 percent of the sexually active gurus had "at least occasional sexual relationships with one or more students."[146] Of the married, many were adulterers and "some are homosexual and some are bisexual in preference."[147] In those cases where gurus had sex with their women disciples, approximately 50 percent of the women were in some way damaged by the incident. Being seduced by the guru was "a source of great suffering."[148]

According to the Associated Press, on June 2, 1986, Guru Prem Paramahansa, 38, was found guilty in Torrance, California, of eight counts of unlawful sex over a 17-month period with an eight-year-old girl (in 1982 and 1983).

The *Chicago Tribune* of August 16, 1982, ran an article on the 400,000-member Ananda Marga Yoga Society titled "Guru Sect is Probed for Terrorism, Murder" and detailing CIA and FBI investigations into the sect. The writer, Bernard Bauer, noted that for 27 years "the cult has left a trail of blood around the world."

To cite a final example, the ISKCON community is currently under federal investigation. Over the years there have been many reports in the *Los Angeles Times* and other papers on alleged criminal activity at the sect's various headquarters; for example, the Gurukula school in Dallas, Texas, and the "New Vrindaban" community in West Virginia. Concerning the latter, the investigative news show "West 57th Street" on October 31, 1987, reported allegations concerning the murder of former members, wife-beating, child-molesting and the sale of illegal drugs, such as cocaine and heroin.

Again, given the forceful denial of absolute standards of right and wrong, is any of the above really so surprising? But there is more. In some forms of Hindu enlightenment, the basic ethical categories of right and wrong must be transcended in another manner—through the *intentional* violation of moral values by the *deliberate* practice of evil.

The goal is to completely erode and ream out the conscience. In that man is created in God's image, and that a strong part of that image involves conscience, it is not surprising that the destruction of the conscience is part of the process of the destruction of the individual. Once the individual and his conscience are reamed out, and only a void remains, is it surprising that what enters and sets up house could be demonic? In other words, the practice of spiritual evil leads to further spiritual evil:

> The effect of this level of practice becomes chillingly clear in the inner rings of the Rajneesh camp.... We see a shockingly effective effort to break down human identity through a calculated violation of the taboos of human morality.... This is more than random vileness. Such thorough-going violation of taboo eventually erodes one's humanity—it "reams out" the physical envelope of a human being and leaves a void where the person should be. This extinction of identity makes possible the entry of demonic entities in a unique and total way.[149]

We emphasize again: To deliberately reject God's handiwork (humanity) as something demonic, and then to proceed to defile it, opens the door to that which truly *is* demonic. And once possessed of evil spirits, anything is possible.

20. Are states of insanity and spirit possession symptoms of higher, divine consciousness and enlightenment?

The gurus themselves frequently admit their own spiritual (i.e., spirit) possession. They also confess that this is their desire for their students. Characteristically, however, such spirit possession is defined in more "spiritual" terms, in light of the respective tradition. For example, it is interpreted as a spiritual manifestation of "enlightenment," as kundalini arousal, as possession by their own gurus' "spiritual form," as "God-possession," as "union with the Divine," etc.

Nevertheless, in the light of historic and biblical demonology, not to mention the guru's own experiences, it is impossible to classify such experiences of possession as divine or spiritual. They are clearly demonic: All the data suggest possession by an evil spirit. (See note 41.)

Unfortunately for the guru, the phenomenon of possession is often accompanied by temporary insanity, usually involving what can only be described as terrible states of madness. Here is one of many links to the tradition of the shaman (and occult magic as well), where the adherents typically encounter possession/insanity as the means to spiritual "enlightenment" and/or authority.[150]

In essence, we believe that the guru is characteristically a type of revolving door for an invading spirit or spirits who come and go as they please, inducing whatever physical, mental, or spiritual phenomena suit their purposes. Below we offer illustrations from leading gurus.

Ramakrishna

During his duties as a priest in the temple of Kali, Ramakrishna went insane:

> Kali was waiting for him. Hardly had he crossed the threshold than divine delirium in its most violent form was rekindled.... The legion of Gods swooped upon him like a whirlwind. He was torn in pieces.... His madness returned tenfold. He saw demonic creatures emerging from him.... Horror paralyzed his limbs.... Two years went by in this orgy of mental intoxication and despair.[151]

Da Free John

In describing his own *sadhana* or work along the spiritual path, Free John openly confesses the insanity of his own gurus. They were indeed mad. They were also possessed by spirits. That Da Free John represents the logical culmination of their teaching and influence speaks for itself. His principal gurus were Nityananda, Muktananda, and Rudrananda ("Rudi"). In *No Remedy*, Da Free John tells of his personal "sanctification":

> Those who have served my function as guru, those who I worked with in my own sadhana, have been wild and powerful men.... True yogis are living, forceful beings. They are madmen, absolutely mad—and absolutely dangerous. You should know that, and you should not approach me if you are not willing to be undone.... My experience with people like Rudi [Rudrananda], Muktananda, Nityananda, and others, was like this: I would be sitting in my house in New York by myself, and this force would enter me, it would practically break my neck, and my body and mind would be taken over.... That is how I learned [of spiritual truth] in these vehicles [gurus].... So these wild men serve that process. And they served it in exactly the same way I serve you. They *acquired* me....[152]

Shree Purohit Swami and Gopi Krishna

Concerning meditation-induced kundalini arousal, a practice of spiritual "enlightenment" often promoted by the gurus, Shree Purohit Swami experienced near-insanity, madly ate the leaves of two entire nimba trees, devoured insipid mudra leaves, and could not sit or stand. He mentions one yogi who had the "fire" rage for six to eight months, and another who had to sit under cold tapwater eight hours a day.[153]

Gopi Krishna, founder of one of the several Kundalini Research Centers in the world, records his own yoga-induced kundalini experiences:

> It was variable for many years, painful, obsessive, even phantasmic. I have passed through almost all the stages of different mediumistic, psychotic and other types of mind, for sometime I was hovering between sanity and insanity. I was writing in many languages, some of which I never knew [the mediumistic ability of automatic writing].[154]

Swami Muktananda

The popular Swami Muktananda described his own possession in some detail in his spiritual autobiography *Play of Consciousness*. In the chapter titled "My Confused State of Mind" and elsewhere he describes this terrible experience

of madness as the "blessing and grace" of his own guru,
Nityananda. Muktananda goes on to state that his disciples
can expect similar experiences, and that such are merely
the normal workings of kundalini arousal:

> By now it is after 9:00. Someone had seated him-
> self in my eyes and was making me see things....It
> seemed that I was being controlled by some power
> which made me do all these things. I no longer had a
> will of my own. My madness was growing all the
> time....My intellect was completely unstable.[155]

Describing his "tandra" state of meditation (an alleged
experience of omniscience), he recalls:

> Every day I had meditation like that. Sometimes
> my body would writhe and twist like a snake's, and a
> hissing sound would come from inside me....Some-
> times my neck moved so violently that it made loud
> cracking sounds, and I became frightened....Some-
> times my neck would roll my head around so vigor-
> ously that it would bend right below my shoulders so
> that I could see my back....Later, however, I learned
> that this was a Hatha Yogic process affected by the
> Goddess Kundalini in order for Her to move up through
> the spinal column....[156]

Swami Rudrananda

> Slowly Swami Nityananda [in spirit form] came
> toward me and entered into my physical body. For
> three hours I felt nothing of myself but that the saint
> had possessed me. It was a terrifying experience and
> it required all my faith not to fight it.[157]

Swami Satchidananda

> I felt myself fall into a sort of trance....I was
> overjoyed with the feeling that my master [Siva-
> nanda] had entered into my own system [body].[158]

Ram Dass

> Some of the times when I'm speaking, it isn't me
> speaking. [I'm not there, my guru] Maharaji was
> teaching you using my body to do it. It would be like
> possession, except that it's an invitational posses-
> sion....He actually moves in and out of my body.[159]

We could continue on down the line, but the point is made: The gurus often admit to possession by an alien spirit being, and accompanying phenomena which often include various forms of madness.

Let us ask you a question: Does what we have been describing so far sound like something divine—or demonic?

Unfortunately, the gurus are not the only ones possessed; the spiritual path they offer to their disciples frequently leads their students to possession as well.[160]

Da (Bubba) Free John

Da (Bubba) Free John (Franklyn Jones) illustrates the state of the disciple being possessed by the alleged "spiritual form" of the guru or master. His text *Garbage and the Goddess* describes the experiences that he and his disciples underwent at his Persimmon, New York, ashram. While Free John describes normal everyday living as being "possessed by the most insidious demonic force in the universe,"[161] one would hardly suspect it from the following descriptions of, as he calls it, "life in God."

Perhaps Free John is correct: "True wisdom is the capacity for perfect madness."[162] Below we cite several descriptions as given by disciples.

> ...the Guru *literally* enters and transforms. It is a kind of possession. It is God-Possession. Bubba animates this body.[163]

> People were screaming and howling and weeping, emitting strange grunts and snarls, their bodies jerking, writhing, and assuming yogic mudras....[164]

> I felt utterly possessed, my body was possessed, and my hands started to move, and I couldn't control them. I had no control at all. My face started taking on expressions.[165]

> My body wasn't mine. I didn't even *feel* my body as mine. There was only this sensation I've had before in Bubba's Presence, the feeling that this body is being used....I went in and at first I was totally out of my mind. I was screaming for a long time....I was making very strange sounds....It is God-possession. It is God totally taking over your form.[166]

> I was so insane I didn't know what was happening at all....[167]

Last night I was led to this spontaneous experience of conducting the force, and I felt possessed, really possessed. Then suddenly I wasn't in my body any more.[168]

Many other gurus also describe their disciples being possessed.

Rudrananda

There are times when the psychic system of the teacher will seem to control the student. He will feel possessed by his teacher. There is nothing to fear from this. It is only a stage of growth through which he [the student] is passing.[169]

Sri Chinmoy

If you remain calm and quiet, and allow your spiritual Guide to enter into you, you will become flooded with Peace. This kind of turning in is not only a valid and correct practice, *but is essential for one who has placed himself under the guidance of a spiritual Master.*[170]

One disciple asked, "During meditation I have the feeling that there is a stranger inside me looking out. It is not me looking out through my eyes, but someone else. Is that usual?" [Chinmoy answers with], "It is quite usual. It is nothing abnormal....It is very healthy good experience, very inspiring."[171]

Bhagwan Shree Rajneesh

Whenever a master wants to help you...he simply possesses you. He simply descends into you....If the disciple is really surrendered, the master can possess him immediately.[172]

21. Is the family unit a detriment to spiritual advancement?

According to many of the Hindu gurus the family unit constitutes a spiritual evil. It engenders too many natural human attachments which of necessity bind one to illusions. Because the family can be so harmful spiritually, the goal for those who are truly committed is to transcend the family—to forsake the family for purposes of enlightenment. Below we consider various statements that reveal some of the Hindu gurus' views toward the family.

Rajneesh

Marriage is the death of love.[173]

Marriage is one of the ugliest institutions man has invented.[174]

The family creates a very, very ill human being.... I am against the family.... If families disappear churches will disappear automatically, because families belong to churches.[175]

Da Free John

Motherhood ... is an illusion. Giving birth is no more divine than taking a crap.... Motherhood is garbage. It is all garbage ... the whole drama of existence ... is garbage.[176]

It is the responsibility of the [spiritual] community to ... continually undermine "marriages."[177]

A.C. Bhakativedanta Prabhupada

No one can be happy in family life.[178]

[Commenting on a verse in the *Srimad Bhagavantam*, Hindu holy literature] During the daytime the wife is compared to a witch and at night she is compared to a tigress. Her only business is sucking the blood of her husband both day and night ... the children are also like tigers, jackals and foxes ... the family members may be called wives and children but actually they are plunderers.[179]

22. What are the personal hazards of Hindu practice?

There are other dangers. When men and women reject their minds, follow religious leaders blindly, undercut and demean moral values, and open themselves to occult forces, it's not surprising that some will be hurt or killed. Some gurus even teach that killing and murder can be "enlightened" actions (cf. notes 180-87). When men and women are taught to see themselves as worthless illusions and to adopt a nihilistic outlook, when they reject moral standards as "unenlightened" and enter abnormal states of consciousness, who can be surprised when there are casualties?

What *is* surprising is the number of people who accept such things as insanity or demonization uncritically, and then naively proceed to interpret them as "true spirituality," "higher consciousness," or "divine enlightenment."

We present the following representative statements concerning possible hazards along the Eastern path.

Rajneesh

> The experience of deep meditation is exactly like death.... [But] when it happens so suddenly, either the body suffers or the mind...some people can go mad.[188]

> This [temporary madness] is going to happen to many. Don't be afraid when it happens.[189]

> Either you will become enlightened or you will go mad—the danger is there. One has to take the risk.[190]

Sri Chinmoy

> Many, many black magicians and people who deal with spirits have been strangled or killed. I know because I have been near quite a few of these cases[191] (cf. note 192).

> I know of a case in India where the hostile forces used to take the form of a particular Master and ask the disciples to commit suicide. "If you commit suicide, I will be able to give you liberation sooner" it would say. They tried to commit suicide even though the Master told them outwardly that he had never said that. These hostile forces are very clever.[193]

Aurobindo

Aurobindo and his co-guru "the Mother" have warned the yoga aspirant of hazards they may face. There may be attacks on them by "cosmic forces"; there are often "disastrous results."[194] The Mother also warns about the hazards of astral projection—here being attacked by other worldly entities who "like amusing themselves at the cost of human beings."[195]

> As soon as they see that someone is not sufficiently protected, they rush in and take possession of the mechanical mind and bring about all kinds of disagreeable happenings—nightmares, various physical disturbances—you feel choked, bite or swallow your tongue and even more serious things.[196]

In conclusion, a brief summarization indicates that to one degree or another many of the gurus in America directly or indirectly:

1. discard the mind and independent thinking;

2. demand an absolute, unquestioning obedience;

3. reject moral standards;

4. demean and cheapen human life as *maya* (illusion);

5. see family life as a perversion or a concession to evil;

6. reject Christianity as a spiritual hazard or abomination;

7. offer teachings leading to despair and nihilism; and

8. offer an occult path that may lead to insanity, serious physical ailments, possession, or death.

Are such teachings truly "Wisdom from the East" or are they really the doctrines of demons referred to in Scripture (1 Timothy 4:1)?

All of this leads to one basic conclusion: Far from dealing with a benevolent form of spirituality or of godly wisdom, "such wisdom does not come down from heaven, but is earthly, unspiritual, of the devil" (James 3:15).

What justifies this assessment? The growing number of tragedies reported by former disciples, including the published accounts of blatant deception, grave immorality, criminal activity, physical assaults, murder and threats of murder, cruelty, drug trafficking, pornography, rapes and other forms of sexual violence—not to mention even worse things on the part of some gurus.[197]

23. What can the followers of Hindu gurus do to inherit eternal life?

Hinduism and Christianity offer people different kinds of salvation. What Hinduism offers men and women is, in the end, complete annihilation—nonexistence. But Jesus Christ offers men and women eternal life—the privilege of knowing and loving a personal God (who loves them) for all eternity.

The Bible teaches us that our sins have separated us from God: "All have sinned and fall short of the glory of God"

(Romans 3:23). Jesus Christ came to die for our sins so that He might freely offer us the gift of eternal life: "The wages of sin is death, but the gift of God is eternal life in Christ Jesus our Lord" (Romans 6:23). Thus "he [Jesus Christ] is the atoning sacrifice for our sins, and not only for ours but also for the sins of the whole world" (1 John 2:2).

Does the guru or spiritual master you now follow truly satisfy your spiritual hunger? Does he claim that he can forgive your sins and give you eternal life? Jesus claims that He can and will. But you must personally receive Him as your Savior. "For God so loved the world that he gave his one and only Son, that whoever believes in him shall not perish but have eternal life" (John 3:16). "To all who received him, to those who believed in his name, he gave the right to become children of God" (John 1:12).

Anyone who desires can receive Christ as his or her personal Savior by saying the following prayer.

Dear God:

I confess before You that I am a sinner and that I cannot earn my own way to heaven. I thank You that You sent Christ to die on the cross for my sins. I now believe that Jesus Christ is the only true Son of God, the only incarnation of God to appear. I now receive Him as my personal Lord and Savior. I ask Christ to come into my life and to make my life pleasing to Him. I also turn from the false path and occult practices that I have accepted. If these practices have led me to be influenced by evil spirits, I ask You to remove them from me. I trust You to protect me from the power of Satan and to glorify Your name in my life. In Jesus' name. Amen.

Notes

1. Stephan Brodian, "Editorial," *Yoga Journal*, July-Aug. 1985, p. 4.
2. Dio Urmilla Neff, "Tumbling from the Pedestal: What Makes Spiritual Teachers Go Renegade?" in *Yoga Journal*, July-Aug. 1985, p. 21.
3. Edward Rice, *Eastern Definitions* (Garden City, NY: Doubleday, 1978), pp. 166-67.
4. Kurt Friedrichs, "Hinduism" in Stephan Schumacher, Gert Woerner, eds., *The Encyclopedia of Eastern Philosophy and Religion* (Boston: Shambhala, 1989), p. 130.
5. Keith Crim, ed., *Abingdon Dictionary of Living Religions* (Nashville: Abingdon, 1981), p. 306.
6. S.G.F. Brandon, ed., *Dictionary of Comparative Religion* (New York: Charles Scribner's Sons, 1970), p. 330.
7. Troy Wilson Organ, *Hinduism* (New York: Baron's Educational Series, 1974), pp. 241-42; Ninian Smart, "Indian Philosophy," in Paul Edward, ed., *The Encyclopedia of Philosophy*, Vol. 4 (New York: Collier-MacMillan, 1973), pp. 155-56; Sarvepalli Radhakrishnan, *Indian Philosophy* (New York: McMillan, 1951, Vol. 2), p. 22; "Vedas," in *Hasting's Encyclopedia of Religion and Ethics*, Vol. 12, p. 597; "India," in *The New Schaff-Herzog Encyclopedia of Religious Knowledge*, Vol. 5, p. 473; Sarvepalli Radhakrishnan and Charles A. Moore, *A Source Book in Indian Philosophy* (Princeton, NJ: Princeton University Press, 1973), p. 506.

44

8. Swami Prabhavananda and Frederick Manchester, *The Spiritual Heritage of India* (New York: Doubleday & Company, 1964), p. 3.

9. Ibid., p. 21

10. Ibid.

11. E.g. Margaret and James Stutley, "Rsi," in *Harper's Dictionary of Hinduism* (New York: Harper & Row, Rev. 1977), p. 251.

12. For an analysis and critique of Transcendental Meditation, see John Weldon and Zola Levitt, *The Transcendental Explosion* (Zola Levitt, Box 12268, Dallas, TX 75225).

13. E.g. consider the influence of Rajneesh, Aurobindo, Ram Dass, Da Free John, Krishnamurti and Yogi Bhajan among many intellectuals, professionals, and students.

14. Roger Walsh, "A Model for Viewing Meditation Research," in the *Journal of Transpersonal Psychology*, Vol. 14, No. 1, 1982, p. 69.

15. These facts are public knowledge freely confessed by knowledgeable members and/or are documented in the author's individual chapters on these subjects in his *Critical Encyclopedia of New Religions and Sects in America*, passim, unpublished. Anyone familiar with Hinduism who thoroughly reads the literature of these groups cannot deny the influence of Hinduism upon them. On the Eckankar plagiarism, see "Eckankar: A Hard Look at a New Religion," in *SCP Journal*, Vol. 3, 1979. On Scientology, see Church of Scientology Information Service, *Scientology: A World Religion Emerges in the Space Age*, Church of Scientology of California, n.p., 1974, pp. 3-8. On Erhard and Muktananda, see the official biography of Erhard by W.W. Bartley III.

16. Ibid.

17. Ibid.

18. Ibid.

19. A.L. Basham, "Hinduism," in R.C. Zaehner, ed., *The Concise Encyclopedia of Living Faiths* (Boston: Beacon Press, 1967), p. 237.

20. "Vedanta," in *Encyclopedia Britannica Micropaedia*, Vol. 10, p. 375.

21. Swami Satprakashananda, *Hinduism and Christianity* (St. Louis: Vedanta Society, 1975), p. 9; cf. Sarvepalli Radhakrishnan, *Indian Philosophy* (New York: MacMillan, 1951, Vol. 2), p. 28.

22. "Vedanta" in *Britannica*, p. 375; Paul Edwards, ed., "Indian Philosophy," in *Encyclopedia of Philosophy*, Vol. 4, pp. 155-56; R. Garbe, "Vedanta," in James Hastings, ed., *Encyclopedia of Religion and Ethics*, Vol. 12, pp. 597-98.

23. See Swami Nikhilananda, "A Discussion of Brahman in the Upanishads," in *The Upanishads, A New Translation, Four Volumes* (New York: Bonanza/Crown Publishers, Harper & Brothers, 1949).

24. *The Oxford American Dictionary* (New York: Avon, 1982), p. 601.

25. Christopher Isherwood, "Introduction," in Christopher Isherwood, ed., *Vedanta for the Western World* (New York: Viking Press, 1968), p. 20.

26. John Yale, ed., *What Religion Is in the Words of Vivekananda?* (New York: The Julian Press, 1962), p. 64.

27. Paramahansa Yogananda, *Man's Eternal Quest* (Los Angeles: Self-Realization Fellowship, 1975), pp. 218-19.

28. Ram Dass, "A Ten-year Perspective," in *The Journal of Transpersonal Psychology*, Vol. 24, No. 2, p. 179.

29. Meher Baba, *Discourses* (San Francisco: Sufism Reoriented, 1973, Vol. 3), p. 146.

30. Bubba Free John, *The Way That I Teach* (Middletown, CA: The Dawn Horse Press, 1978), pp. 226, 227, 238-48.

31. Bhagwan Shree Rajneesh, "Society Is an Illusion," in *Sannyas*, No. 2, 1979, pp. 3-5.

32. Bhagwan Shree Rajneesh, *I Am the Gate* (San Francisco: Perennial Library, 1978), pp. 5-6.

33. Robert A. McDermott, ed., *The Essential Aurobindo* (New York: Schocken Books, 1974), p. 24.

34. John, *Teach*, p. 239; cf. pp. 238-48.

35. Bertrand Russell, *Why I Am Not a Christian and Other Essays* (New York: Simon & Schuster/Touchstone, 1957), p. 107.

36. Mahendranath Gupta, *The Gospel of Sri Ramakrishna* (New York: Ramakrishna-Vivekananda Center, 1977), p. 405.

37. Reprint of "Oh Benares" article from *National Review* in *SCP Newsletter*, 1985, p. 22.

38. Primary references are supplied in John Ankerberg and John Weldon, *Can You Trust Your Doctor? The Complete Guide to New Age Medicine and Its Threat to Your Family* (Brentwood, TN: Wolgemuth & Hyatt, 1991), pp. 287-301.

39. Ibid., pp. 146-47.

40. Erika Bourguignon, *Religion, Altered States of Consciousness and Social Change* (Columbus, OH: Ohio State University Press, 1973), pp. 16-17.

41. Tal Brooke, with research assistance by John Weldon, *Riders of the Cosmic Circuit* (Batavia, IL: Lion Publishers, 1986), pp. 39-50, 107-39, 165-208; available from Spiritual Counterfeits Project, P.O. Box 4308, Berkeley, CA 94702.

42. "Meditation," in Ankerberg and Weldon, *Trust*, Chapter 10.

43. Gopi Krishna, "The True Aim of Yoga," in *Psychic* magazine, Jan.-Feb. 1973, p. 14.

44. Ibid., p. 15.

45. Stanislav Grof and Christina Grof, eds., *Spiritual Emergency: When Personal Transformation Becomes a Crisis* (Los Angeles: Jeremy P. Tarcher, 1989).

46. Moti Lal Pandit, "Yoga As Methods of Liberation," in *Update: A Quarterly Journal on New Religious Movements* (Aarhus, Denmark: The Dialogue Center, Vol. 9, No. 4, Dec. 1985), p. 41.

47. John Ankerberg and John Weldon, *The Facts on the Occult* and *The Facts on Spirit Guides* (Eugene, OR: Harvest House, 1991).

48. Swami Prabhavananda, *Yoga and Mysticism* (Hollywood, CA: Vedanta Press, 1972), pp. 18-19.

49. E.g. Ernest Wood, *Seven Schools of Yoga: An Introduction* (Wheaton, IL: Theosophical Publishing House, 1973), pp. 77, 79.

50. Bhagwan Shree Patanjali (translation and commentary by Shree Purohit Swami), *Aphorisms of Yoga* (London: Faber & Faber, 1972), pp. 56-57.

51. Sri Chinmoy, *Astrology, the Supernatural and the Beyond* (Jamaica, NY: Agni Press, 1973), pp. 53-68, 87-89; Sri Chinmoy, *Conversations with the Master* (Jamaica, NY: Agni Press, 1977), pp. 9-20, 26-33.

52. Sri Chinmoy, *Great Masters and the Cosmic Gods* (Jamaica, NY: Agni Press, 1977), p. 8.

53. Hans Ulrich-Rieker, *The Yoga of Light: Hatha Yoga Pradipika* (New York: Seabury Press), 1971, pp. 9, 134.

54. Krishna, "Aim," p. 13.

55. Ulrich-Rieker, *Yoga*, p. 79.

56. Sri Krishna Prem, *The Yoga of the Bhagavat Gita* (Baltimore: Penguin, 1973), p. xv.

57. Ibid., p. 47.

58. Swami Prabhavananda, *Yoga and Mysticism* (Hollywood, CA: Vedanta Press, 1972), pp. 18-19.

59. Ulrich-Rieker, *Yoga*, pp. 30, 79, 96, 111-12.

60. Wood, *Seven Schools*, p. 14.

61. Brooks Alexander, "Book Review: *Riders of the Cosmic Circuit*," in *SCP Journal*, Vol. 7, No. 1, 1987, p. 39.

62. Bhagwan Shree Rajneesh in Swami Anand Yarti, *The Sound of Running Water: A Photobiography of Bhagwan Sri Rajneesh and His Work 1974-1978* (Poona, India: Poona Rajneesh Foundation, 1980), p. 364.

63. Daniel Goleman, "The Buddha on Meditation and States of Consciousness," in Charles Tart, ed., *Transpersonal Psychologies* (New York: Harper Colophon Books, 1977), p. 218.

64. Swami Muktananda, *Play of Consciousnes* (New York: Harper & Row, 1978), pp. xxiii, 155-61.

65. Paramahansa Yogananda, *Autobiography of a Yogi* (Los Angeles: Self-Realization Fellowship, 1972), pp. 16, 55-57, 132, 137, 190, 475-79.

66. Paramahansa Yogananda, "Where Are Our Departed Loved Ones?" in *Self-Realization Magazine*, Spring 1978, pp. 6-7.

67. *Sri Aurobindo and the Mother on Occultism*, compiled by Vijay (Pondicherry, India: Sri Aurobindo Society, 1972), p. 17.

68. Sri Aurobindo, *A Practical Guide to Integral Yoga*, compiled by Manishai (Pondicherry, India: Sri Aurobindo Ashram, 1973), p. 273.

69. Nikhilananda, "Discussion."

70. Swami Nikhilananda, *The Gospel of Sri Ramakrishna*, Sixth Edition (New York: Ramakrishna-Vivekananda Center, 1977), p. 395.

71. Swami Nikhilananda, *Vivekananda, the Yogas and Other Works* (New York: Ramakrishna-Vivekananda Center, 1953), p. 355.

72. Nikhilananda, *Gospel*, p. 102.

73. Ibid., p. 218.

74. Nikhilananda, *Vivekananda*, p. 740.

75. Yale, *Religion*, pp. 195, 199-200.

76. Swami Vivekananda, *Teachings of Swami Vivekananda* (Calcutta, India: Swami Budhananda, 1975), pp. 91-92.

77. Swami Muktananda, *Siddha Meditation: Commentaries on the Shiva Sutras and Other Sacred Texts by Swami Muktananda* (Oakland, CA: Siddha Yoga Dham of America Foundation, 1975), pp. 98-99; cf. pp. 103-06.

78. Swami Muktananda, *Mukteshwari*, Part 2 (Ganeshpuri, India: Shree Gurudev Ashram, 1973), p. 158.

79. Swami Muktananda, *American Tour 1970* (Piedmont, CA: Shree Gurudev Siddha Yoga Ashram, 1974), p. 5.

80. Swami Muktananda, *Play of Consciousness* (San Francisco: Harper & Row, 1974), pp. 203-04.

81. Swami Satchidananda, *An Evening with Swami Satchidananda* (New York: Integral Yoga Institute, 1974), p. 6 (pamphlet).

82. Sathya Sai Baba, *Sathyam-Shivam Sundaram*, Part 3 (Bangalore, India: Sri Sathya Sai Publication and Education Foundation, 1973), p. 112.

83. Sathya Sai Baba, *Sathya Sai Speaks*, Vol. 9 (Bangalore, India: Sri Sathya Sai Publication and Education Foundation, n.d.), p. 68.

84. Ibid., p. 184.

85. Bhagwan Shree Rajneesh, *The Mustard Seed* (San Francisco: Harper & Row, 1975), p. 362.

46

86. Swami Vishnudevananda, *The Complete Illustrated Book of Yoga* (New York: Pocket Books, 1972), p. 351.
87. Bhagwan Shree Rajneesh, *The Rajneesh Bible*, Vol. 1 (Rajneeshpuram, OR: Rajneesh Foundation International, 1985), pp. 9-10.
88. Ibid., pp. 26-27.
89. Nikhilananda, *Vivekananda*, p. 511.
90. Vivekananda in Yale, *Religion*, p. xii.
91. Da Free John, *Scientific Proof of the Existence of God Will Soon Be Announced at the White House* (Clearlake Highlands, CA: The Dawnhorse Press, 1980), p. 212.
92. Da Free John, *The Enlightenment of the Whole Body* (Clearlake Highlands, CA: The Dawnhorse Press, 1978), p. 412.
93. John Ankerberg and John Weldon, *The Case for Jesus the Messiah* and *Do the Resurrection Accounts Conflict and What Proof Is There Jesus Rose from the Dead?* (Chattanooga, TN: Ankerberg Theological Research Institute, 1989 and 1990).
94. Bhagwan Shree Rajneesh, *I Am the Gate* (New York: Harper & Row/Perennial, 1977), p. 16.
95. Ian Stevenson, *Twenty Cases Suggestive of Reincarnation*, Second Edition, rev. (Charlottesville, VA: University Press of Virginia, 1978), pp. 374-77.
96. Walter Martin, *The Riddle of Reincarnation*; John Snyder, *Reincarnation Versus Resurrection* (Chicago: Moody Press, 1984), pp. 38-41; Mark Albrecht, *Reincarnation: A Christian Appraisal* (Downer's Grove, IL: InterVarsity, 1982), pp. 71-78; Norman L. Geisler and J. Yutaka Amano, *The Reincarnation Sensation* (Wheaton, IL: Tyndale, 1987), pp. 78, 82; Robert A. Morey, *Reincarnation and Christianity* (Minneapolis: Bethany, 1980), pp. 24-30, passim.
97. Sri Aurobindo, *The Mother* (Pondicherry, India: Sri Aurobindo Ashram, 1977), p. 3.
98. Bhagwan Shree Rajneesh, "This Is Not a Democracy," in *Sannyas*, No. 4, 1978, p. 33.
99. Sathya Sai Baba, *Sathya Sai Speaks*, Vol. 2 (Bangalore, India: Sri Sathya Sai Publication and Education Foundation, n.d.), p. 186.
100. As given by Baba's principal biographer, C.B. Purdom, *The God-Man* (London: George Allen and Unwin, 1964), p. 351; although a committed disciple of Sai Baba and his leading biographer, Purdom warns against excessive obedience.
101. *Oregon Magazine* (Portland), Sept. 1984, p. 66; *Los Angeles Times*, Mar. 18, 1979.
102. Bubba (Da) Free John, *No Remedy—Revised and Enlarged Edition* (Lowerlake, CA: The Dawn Horse Press, 1976), p. 276.
103. Bhagwan Shree Rajneesh as cited in Vasant Joshi, *The Awakened One: The Life and Work of Bhagwan Shree Rajneesh* (San Francisco: Harper & Row, 1982), p. 80.
104. Bhagwan Shree Rajneesh as cited in Ma Satya Bharti, *Drunk on the Divine: An Account of Life in the Ashram of Bhagwan Shree Rajneesh* (New York: Grove Press, 1981), pp. 52, 150.
105. Bhagwan Shree Rajneesh, "In the Cave of the Heart Is Freedom," in *Sannyas*, No. 5, 1979, p. 15.
106. Sathya Sai Baba interview in Samuel Sandweiss, *Sai Baba: The Holy Man and the Psychiatrist* (San Diego: Birth Day Publishing, 1975), p. 206.
107. Sai Baba, *Speaks*, Vol. 4, p. 15.
108. Sai Baba, *Speaks*, Vol. 7, p. 473.
109. Meher Baba, *The Path of Love* (New York: Samuel Wiser, 1976), p. 38.
110. Satprem, *Sri Aurobindo or the Adventure of Consciousness* (New York: Harper & Row, 1968), p. 44.
111. Lakh Raj Puri, *Radha Swami Teachings* (Punjab, India: K.L. Khanna, Secretary, Radha Soami Satsang Beas, 1972), p. 41.
112. Charan Singh, *Light on St. Matthew* (Punjab, India: Shri S.L. Sondhi, Secretary, Radha Soami Satsang Beas, 1979), p. 128.
113. Gita Mehta, *Karma Cola: The Marketing of the Mystic East* (New York: Simon & Schuster, 1979), pp. 18-19.
114. Bhagwan Shree Rajneesh, "Simple, Utterly Simple," in *Sannyas*, No. 5, 1980, p. 38.
115. Bhagwan Shree Rajneesh, "Pulling Out Weeds," in *Sannyas*, No. 5, 1980, p. 5.
116. Rajneesh, *Bible*, Vol. 1, p. 79.
117. Maharishi Mahesh Yogi, *Transcendental Meditation* (New York: New American Library, 1968), p. 99.
118. Yogananda, *Quest*, pp. 11, 178.
119. Rajneesh, *Mustard*, p. 200.
120. Rajneesh, *Gate*, p. 1.
121. Bhagwan Shree Rajneesh, "Why Don't You Help Me to Become Enlightened?" in *Sannyas*, No. 1, 1978, p. 16; cf. p. 18.
122. Bubba Free John, *Garbage and the Goddess* (Lowerlake, CA: The Dawn Horse Press, 1974), pp. 310-11.
123. George Feuerstein and Jeanine Miller, *Yoga and Beyond: Essays in Indian Philosophy* (New York: Shocken Books, 1972), p. 8.
124. Bhagwan Shree Rajneesh, "I Am the Messiah, Here and Now," in *Sannyas*, No. 5, 1978, p. 34.
125. Bhagwan Shree Rajneesh as quoted in "Editorial—The Living Master," in *Sannyas*, No. 4, 1980, p. 3.
126. Bhagwan Shree Rajneesh, "God Is a Christ in a Christ," in *Sannyas*, No. 3, 1978, p. 11.

127. John, *Garbage*, pp. 10-12.
128. Ibid., p. 23.
129. Bubba [Da] Free John, *No Remedy*, rev. ed., 1976, p. 274.
130. William Rodamor, "The Secret Life of Swami Muktananda," in *Co-Evolution Quarterly*, Winter 1983, p. 110.
131. Muktananda, *Meditation*, p. 34; Mukatananda, *Mukteshwri*, Part 2, p. 29.
132. Sita Wiener, *Swami Satchidananda* (San Francisco: Straight Arrow Books, 1970), p. 156.
133. Yogananda, *Quest*, p. 332.
134. Rajneesh in Yarti, *Sound*, p. 382.
135. Rajneesh, *Bible*, Vol. 1, p. 368.
136. Rajneesh, "Messiah," in *Sannyas*, Sep.-Oct. 1978, p. 34.
137. Rajneesh in Yarti, *Sound*, p. 153.
138. Bhagwan Shree Rajneesh, *The Book of the Secrets*, Vol. 1 (San Francisco: Harper-Colophon Books, 1974), p. 22.
139. John, *Garbage*, p. 18.
140. Swami Adbhutananda, "Brahman and Maya," in Christopher Isherwood, ed., *Vedanta for the Western World*, p. 160.
141. Nikhilananda, *Vivekananda*, p. 512.
142. Rajneesh Bharti, *Drunk*, p. 35.
143. John, *No Remedy*, pp. 52-53; cf. p. 55.
144. John, *Garbage*, pp. 32-33.
145. Jack Kornfield, "Sex Lives of the Gurus," in *Yoga Journal*, July-Aug. 1985, p. 28.
146. Ibid., p. 27.
147. Ibid., pp. 27-28.
148. Ibid., p. 28.
149. Alexander, "Book Review," p. 39.
150. I.M. Lewis, *Ecstatic Religion: An Anthropological Study of Spirit Possession and Shamanism*, 1975; Michael Harner, "The Sound of Rushing Water," in Harner, ed., *Hallucinogens and Shamanism*, pp. 17, 20, and his *The Way of the Shaman*, 1986; Mircea Eliade, *Shamanism: Archaic Techniques of Ecstasy*, 1974; Robert S. Ellwood, *Religious and Spiritual Groups in Modern America* (Englewood Cliffs, NJ: Prentice Hall, 1973), p. 12; David Conway, *Magic: An Occult Primer* (New York: Bantam, 1975), pp. 129-32.
151. Romain Rolland, *The Life of Ramakrishna* (Calcutta, India: Advaita Ashrama, trans. from the original French by E.F. Malcolm-Smith, 1979), p. 41.
152. John, *No Remedy*, rev. ed., pp. 174-76.
153. Bhagwan Shree Patanjali, *Aphorisms of Yoga*, trans. Shree Purohit Swami (London: Faber & Faber, 1973), pp. 58-59.
154. Gopi Krishna, *The Awakening of Kundalini* (New York: Dutton, 1975), p. 124.
155. Muktananda, *Consciousness*, p. 76; cf. pp. 75-89.
156. Ibid., pp. 88-89.
157. Rudi (Swami Rudrananda), *Spiritual Cannibalism* (Woodstock, NY: The Overlook Press, 1978), p. 13.
158. Wiener, *Swami*, pp. 119-20.
159. Ram Dass Interview, *New Age Journal*, No. 9, p. 27; interview, *The Movement* magazine, 1976.
160. Cf. note 41; T. George Harris editorial in *Psychology Today*, Dec. 1975, p. 4.
161. John, *Garbage*, p. 51.
162. Da Free John, *A New Tradition: An Introduction to the Laughing Man Institute and The Crazy Wisdom Fellowship* (n.p., The Laughing Man Institute, 1980), p. 1.
163. John, *Garbage*, p. 151.
164. Ibid., pp. 71-72.
165. Ibid., p. 263.
166. Ibid., pp. 282-83, 285.
167. Ibid., p. 66.
168. Ibid., p. 312.
169. Rudrananda, *Cannibalism*, p. 103.
170. Sri Chinmoy, *Yoga and the Spiritual Life* (Jamaica, NY: Agni Press, 1974), p. 113, emphasis added.
171. Sri Chinmoy, "Questions and Answers," in *Aum* magazine, Jan. 1980, p. 23.
172. Rajneesh in Yarti, *Sound*, p. 168.
173. Rajneesh, *Bible*, Vol. 1, p. 406.
174. Ibid., p. 416.
175. Ibid., pp. 11, 14-15.
176. John, *Garbage*, pp. 119-20.
177. Ibid., pp. 7-8.
178. Swami A.C. Bhaktivedanta Prabhupada, *Srimad Bhaghavantam*, Fifth Canto, Part Two (Los Angeles: Bhaktivedanta Book Trust, 1975), p. 230.
179. Ibid., p. 101.
180. Rajneesh, *Secrets*, Vol. 1, p. 399.
181. Ibid., p. 69.

182. Swami Rama, *Life Here and Hereafter* (Glenview, IL: Himalayan National Institute, 1976), p. 67.

183. Nikhilananda, *Vivekananda*, p. 530.

184. A.C. Bhaktivedanta Prabhupada, *Bhaghavad-gita As It Is* (New York: Collier Books, 1973), Chapter 9, verse 30, p. 483; cf. *Back to Godhead*, No. 55, p. 25.

185. *Bhaghavad Gita*, Chapter 18, verse 17.

186. Maharishi Mahesh Yogi, *Maharishi Mahesh Yogi on the Bhaghavad Gita—A New Translation and Commentary with Sanskrit Text—Chapters 1-6* (Baltimore: Penguin Books, 1969), p. 26.

187. *The Kaushitaki* Upanishad 3:1-2.

188. Bhagwan Shree Rajneesh, *Hammer on the Rock: A Darshan Diary* (New York: Grove Press, 1978), p. 371; cf. p. 373.

189. Rajneesh, "Christ," in *Sannyas*, No. 3, 1978, p. 11.

190. Bhagwan Shree Rajneesh, "Energy," in *Sannyas*, No. 1, 1978, p. 5.

191. Chinmoy, *Astrology*, p. 62.

192. Ibid., p. 71.

193. Ibid., p. 94.

194. Aurobindo, *Guide*, p. 142; Sri Aurobindo and the Mother, *On Occultism*, p. 2.

195. Aurobindo and the Mother, *On Occultism*, p. 2.

196. Ibid., pp. 18-19.

197. See e.g. Tal Brooke, *Lord of the Air* (Eugene, OR: Harvest House, 1990); Ram Dass, "Egg on My Beard," in *The Yoga Journal*, Nov.-Dec. 1976, also July-Aug. 1985; Peter Marin, "Spiritual Obedience," in *Harpers* magazine, Feb. 1979; "The Secret Life of Swami Muktananda," in *Co-Evolution Quarterly*, Winter 1983; *The (Portland) Oregonian*, Dec. 30, 1985; and Brooke, *Riders*, for illustrations in the lives of many prominent gurus; see also the two books by Bharti.